Anxiety

A Manual For Managing Your Emotions And Stopping
Overthinking: A Guide To Overcoming Negative
Thoughts, Stress, Anxiety, And Toxic Emotions

(Equip Yourself With Knowledge To Alleviate Anxiety)

Bernard Turnbull

TABLE OF CONTENT

Comparing Social Anxiety In Men And Women 1

How Do The Body And Mind Work Together?11

Preventing Adverse Attachment Vulnerability
....16

Can You Benefit From The Success Triangle?.22

When To Get Expert Assistance 33

Stress And Time Management...............................51

Simplifying Your Life To Streamline Your
Lifestyle For Mental Clarity......................................72

How To Make Worrying Useful 98

Uncertainty In Partnerships 104

Comparing Social Anxiety In Men And Women

Studies reveal that social anxiety is experienced differently by men and women. First of all, compared to men, women tend to be more socially apprehensive. Throughout their lives, women are more likely than males to experience social anxiety (5.67% vs 4.20%). Furthermore, compared to men, women who experience social anxiety have poorer psychosocial functioning. According to Xu et al. (2012), social anxiety impedes women's capacity to build meaningful social interactions and carry out their everyday tasks with efficiency.

One noteworthy distinction between genders is that women are more likely than males to have social anxiety in the office or in any setting where they must deal with superiors. On the other hand, dating-related problems are the primary cause of anxiety among men (Xu et al., 2012).

Given that anxiety typically manifests in a variety of ways, including symptoms and comorbidities, researchers have attempted to determine if men and women experience anxiety in these ways differently. For instance, women experience higher levels of anxiety and more severe symptoms than males do when they are socially anxious. They also run a higher risk of acquiring PTSD, Generalized Anxiety Disorder, and specific phobias associated with social situations. Contrarily, men are more likely to acquire substance abuse disorders and conduct disorder, which is defined by negative emotional behavior and disdain for others (Asher &Aderka, 2018).

Experts surmise several factors, including the societal conditioning that both men and women experience, may contribute to these disparities. Some actions are thought to be more suitable for women than for men. Systemic problems and a lack of psychological safety are two other factors that might exacerbate anxiety. Researchers are also attempting to determine whether variations in brain chemistry may contribute to gender disparities in social anxiety behaviors. The following will discover more about women and social anxiety.

The Social Anxiety Cognitive Model

Over the years, academics have developed various models to understand better how social anxiety may impact our cognitive abilities. Developed in 1995, the Clark and Wells model is one of the most well-known and traditional models. Most subsequent models also share many of the topics covered in this model.

This hypothesis suggests that those who suffer from social anxiety overwork themselves to appear flawless. Put another way, they think they must be flawless to form deep social bonds with other people. Ironically, their preoccupation with being flawless can increase their anxiety and cause them to perform worse than normal.

The fact that most socially anxious individuals are incessantly self-aware in evaluating their social performance—that is, they focus more on their own emotions than on other people's outward actions and reactions—is another significant feature of social anxiety. They may believe, for instance, that "I'm coming across as awkward and nervous" or "People think I'm acting strangely." People who struggle with social anxiety may find these claims genuine, but they may not bother to verify them. People may not be laughing at them or thinking that they are socially uncomfortable, for instance, but they are unaware of this because they are unwilling to let go of their thoughts.

People who struggle with social anxiety are generally not open to learning new things, especially when they originate from outside sources. If they ever pay attention to or listen to anything, it will always be something that feeds into their poor perception of themselves. For instance, if they believe that others can tell how anxious they are and someone asks them casually whether they are okay, they may conclude that their anxiety is quite obvious.

As you can see, these thought patterns frequently serve as self-fulfilling prophecies, with each error appearing to confirm how they truly view themselves. Furthermore, individuals need more opportunities to disprove their ideas because they rarely attempt to do so through social interaction.

We will go into more depth on safety and avoidant behaviors near the end of the chapter, as they are a key component of the cognitive model.

Meditation and relaxation techniques

Pose

Yoga uses various postural and breathing practices to restore harmony and balance to the body and emotions.

There are several ways to use systematic relaxation to help you manage stress.

Even though classes are the greatest place to learn meditation and relaxation techniques.

Numerous relaxation techniques exist, from audio CDs to group martial arts and fitness classes.

These are just a few examples of the kinds of structured activities that are available to help increase our ability to relax:

Autogenic instruction

This method, created in the early 20th century, emphasizes awareness of physical sensations and passive attention.

Repetition of so-called autogenic "formulas" allows one to focus on specific sensations, such as heat or weight in certain body parts.

Clinicians have used autogenic training as part of the treatment of many disorders.

This method, well-liked in Europe and even covered by some insurance policies, is progressively gaining traction in the US.

No particular physical requirements or workouts are required; nonetheless, individuals who wish to learn this technique should be ready to invest patience and time.

This method is far more advanced than some relaxation techniques; therefore, taking a course is usually the best way to familiarize oneself.

Biofeedback is a method that uses monitoring equipment to provide information from the body that would not otherwise be available to teach people how to relax, control stress reactions, or modify their behavior.

The underlying idea of this approach was first put forth in the early 1960s: the autonomic nervous system, or the part of our nervous system that is not consciously used, is trainable.

Devices might be used, for instance, to measure blood pressure, heart rate, brain activity, stomach acidity, muscle tension, and other parameters. At the same time, people experiment with different breathing techniques, thought patterns, or postures.

By acquiring this information, one can pinpoint the mechanisms that result in the desired outcome, like a reduction in blood pressure and heart rate.

Many practitioners use biofeedback to treat a variety of psychological and physical conditions.

Picture:

Using relaxing or pleasant images to soothe the body and mind is known as imaging, sometimes guided imagery.

Deep relaxation can be attained by controlling breathing and visualizing an enjoyable scene.

Healthy Eating

What Is Balanced Eating? Balanced eating, also known as a balanced diet or balanced nutrition, is a way of consuming food that entails making deliberate and thoughtful decisions to give the body the nutrients it needs for the best possible physical and mental health.

Produce and Fruits:

Packed with Nutrients: Vegetables and fruits are

Mood Support: They improve general health and include nutrients connected to mood management, like vitamin C and folate.

Diversity: An array of vibrant fruits and vegetables guarantees a wide range of nutrients.

Complete Grains:

Complex Carbohydrates: Whole grains that provide long-lasting energy include brown rice, oats, quinoa, and whole wheat.

Fiber: Their high dietary fiber content promotes healthy digestion and stable blood sugar levels.

The protein

Lean Sources: Lean proteins, including those found in fish, chicken, lentils, tofu, and lean meat cuts, provide the essential amino acids needed to synthesize neurotransmitters.

Proteins aid in the sensation of fullness, which helps to curb overeating.

Nutritious Fats:

Unsaturated Fats: Good fat sources for the brain include avocados, almonds, seeds, and olive oil.

Hydration: Cognitive Function: Sustaining general well-being and cognitive function depends on maintaining adequate hydration.

Electrolyte equilibrium: Staying properly hydrated promotes electrolyte balance and aids in the body's physiological functions.

Effect on Anxiety: Eating a balanced diet is important for managing anxiety for several reasons.

Nutrient Sufficiency: Eating a balanced diet guarantees that the body gets all the nutrients it needs, including those critical for creating neurotransmitters and brain function.

Stable Blood Sugar: It aids in maintaining stable blood sugar levels, which helps to avoid mood swings and lessens the feelings of anxiety brought on by blood sugar changes.

Physical Wellbeing: Mental and physical well-being are intimately related. Nutrient-dense diets promote general health, which positively impacts mental health.

Satiety: Consuming enough protein and fiber helps one feel full and inhibits overindulging, which lowers the chance of emotional eating brought on by worry.

Making decisions that promote general health and well-being rather than adhering to rigid diets or deprivation is the goal of balanced eating. Giving the body and mind the vital nutrients they require to flourish can greatly aid in the holistic management of anxiety when paired with mindful eating practices.

How Do The Body And Mind Work Together?

In this fourth and penultimate of the book, I wish to introduce a subject that both philosophy professionals and psychology scholars find important. What link there is between the mind and the body is the main topic of discussion between the two disciplines on a frequent basis in this chapter.

I will start by laying out the ideas that attempt to explain how the body and the mind are related in order to respond to your issue. Next, I will address a really delicate query: may unfavorable ideas contribute to the development of illness? Or, in this instance, does the mind have no effect on the body? Ultimately, I will impart all of my understanding of the connection between the mind and body to assist you in achieving the much-needed mental and physical health. It takes calmness and optimistic thinking to reach this equilibrium! Continue reading if you want to learn more about the topic and at last put an end to your overanalysis.

Theories that describe how the body and mind interact

Philosophers and scientists have been captivated by the link between the mind and body for a minimum of two millennia. The ancient Greek philosophers are, in fact, the ones who gave us the first theories that systematically linked mind and body. Let's examine the primary theoretical stances that can be adopted in relation to this matter.

I want to introduce you to monism, which is a theory regarding the link between the body and the mind. According to this view, the mind and body are made of the same substance and cannot be distinguished from one another. The human mind and psyche are composed of physical substance, just as the body, including the brain, is a physical entity. This idea has the clear advantage of being clear-cut and accurate without requiring the existence of something as "peculiar" as an unseen mental dimension. Nonetheless, the primary problem with monism is that it is hard to believe that the mind and body are the same physical entities! Since the human mind is multifaceted and cannot be reduced to a physical substance, monism is therefore frequently argued in more sophisticated and nuanced forms these days. Two distinct forms of monism exist. The first version holds that there is only the brain and that the idea of "mind" should be completely abolished because it is wholly abstract. This is why the philosophy is known as "eliminativism." This form of monism holds that the psychic or spiritual realm is merely human "fantasy" and that everything that exists is wholly physical. Another, considerably more restrained kind of monism exists as well. We refer to this alternative form of monism as "reductionism." Reductionism holds that the physical dimension—that is, the dimension proper to the brain—should include the mental and psychic dimensions in its entirety. Reductionism does not advocate dispelling the mind as if it were untrue or a delusion. It does, however, make the case that everything that we consider to be "psyche" need to be limited to the material realm.

I want to introduce you to the second theory, which is known as dualism. As the name also implies, dualism is the opposite of monism. Dualism asserts the presence of two distinct substances, whereas monism holds that the mind and the body are composed of the same (physical) material. The physical material, which includes the brain in particular, is on the one hand, and the psychological or spiritual substance is on the other. One significant benefit of dualism is that it upholds our shared beliefs regarding the "obvious" differences between the mind and the body. Unfortunately, dualism also has a significant drawback: it is unable to provide a persuasive explanation for how the mind and the body, two distinct entities, connect with one another. Though some theories have been proposed (such the pineal gland's ability to "bind together" thoughts and body matter), the majority of scientists have not been persuaded by them thus far.

You studied about a few theories in the first paragraph that describe how the mind and body interact. We might also inquire about the possibility of negative mind-body influence in relation to this notion. Specifically, is it possible for negative thinking to contribute to the development of illness? If you want the answers, continue reading.

Preventing Adverse Attachment Vulnerability

In the context of attachment, avoidant attachment is a method of emotional self-sufficiency. In this environment, a child may come across caregivers who are emotionally aloof or insensitive to their needs. These children learn to cope with emotional detachment by prioritizing autonomy and self-sufficiency, often at the expense of their own emotional needs.

Avoidantly attached people frequently find emotional connection uncomfortable and may struggle to express their needs or feelings openly. They usually keep a distance in their interactions and prioritize autonomy over sensitivity. Their self-soothing and emotional independence histories have given them a self-reliance that may be both a strength and a weakness when it comes to forging close, personal ties.

HOW EARLY CONNECTIONS FORM ATTACHMENT

One of the essential aspects of human psychology, attachment formation, starts in the womb. It is a journey defined by the interactions between children and their primary caregivers, beginning in the tender embrace of childhood. These formative relationships act as a nursery for attachment styles, subsequently impacting individuals' social interactions later in life. We must first look at these formative experiences' crucial elements to completely comprehend the connection between childhood experiences and attachment styles.

1. Responsiveness of Caregiver

Secure connection: In the event of a secure connection, caregivers regularly respond to an infant's needs with warmth, affection, and emotional awareness. Securely attached children grow to depend on their caregivers for consolation and assistance. By forming a strong conviction that their wants will be met, they lay the groundwork for their secure attachment type.

Anxious Attachment: When a child has an anxious attachment, caregivers might not always react to their emotional cues. A youngster may become anxious and insecure due to inconsistent behavior. They could learn that their caregivers' reactions come as a surprise, which makes them more cautious and reliant on comfort.

2. Regularity And Predictability

Secure Attachment: The child feels stable when caregivers are consistent in their methods and emotionally receptive. Youngsters who have strong connections develop an expectation of consistency in the behavior of their caretakers. Because they know they can always return to a safe base, this sense of security enables them to explore their surroundings and grow into healthy, independent individuals.

Anxious Attachment: Loss of stability and predictability can be emotionally upsetting for people who have an anxious attachment. They could find it hard to trust people in partnerships because they think their emotional needs will not be met on a regular basis. Uncertainty can lead to clinginess and an overwhelming need for regular reassurance.

How to Meditate for Inner Peace

Meditation is the ideal mental substitute for developing calm if physical activity appears too demanding. Allow me to introduce you to the many contemporary types of meditation that exist, before you roll your eyes and assume that meditation is limited to incense, chanting, and hours spent sitting cross-legged in quiet. Fundamentally, meditation is just directing your attention in particular directions to calm your thoughts and increase awareness. Indeed, it has the power to alter lives.

Using phone apps that offer brief, guided meditations for beginners, such as Calm, Headspace, or Insight Timer, is a terrific place to start. Shut your eyes, begin with just 5–10 minutes each day, and adhere to the calming instructions. Being consistent is crucial. Consider it similar to gaining muscle: you begin with little weights and progressively raise the effort.

Focus on breathing, reciting a mantra, or performing a body scan while meditating. When thoughts do come to pass, do not be critical of yourself. Bring your attention back to your anchor. Your capacity for sustained concentration is growing. Rumination on the past and concern about the future are two mental traps that exacerbate anxiety; by grounding oneself in the present, these tendencies are released.

Establishing meditation first thing in the morning sets up your nervous system to experience less tension and anxiety during the day. Like coffee for the mind, only without the jitters! You should also meditate before bed for a more peaceful night's sleep. Think about burning a candle or diffusing aromatic oils to create a calming ambiance.

Many people find traditional seated poses beneficial, but you can also try lying down, strolling meditation, or even contemplative coloring. Make your practice unique to ensure sustainability. You can eventually extend awareness to routine tasks like taking a shower, preparing meals, and cleaning your teeth.

Thus, do not be afraid to get going! Make a loving intention and practice self-compassion. Consider it mental exercise; you are strengthening your capacity for unwavering, impartial awareness. Regular meditation practice yields compounding benefits that permeate your everyday existence.

Can You Benefit From The Success Triangle?

If, like me and a few billion other people, your worried imagination is always racing forward, imagining a place that will make you feel wonderful on the inside out. This small tool helps give structure to that unknown future.

Self-indulgent rewards could provide us happiness for a short while, but they never satisfy the emptiness inside. But as soon as you fill that hole, your loving heart takes precedence over your worried mind because it now has a concrete north star to guide it.

Having distributed this tool to hundreds of individuals worldwide, I've realized that all setups are unique. Your Golden Mission, like your thumbprint, is exclusive to you.

So, will you find it effective?

Here is what I can say for sure, however.

I am still using this tool five years after I made it. My second and third basic needs have evolved during that period, just as your strategy and objectives do. Yet my motivation—my fundamental need—hasn't changed.

After removing the poisonous mist of uncertainty and not knowing what I was meant to be doing with my life throughout those five years, I am now living life with clarity, confidence, and a constant sense of fulfillment.

When my thoughts, words, and actions are in harmony, I feel both inspired and at ease. This is where the Triangle of Success comes in. Making objectives and plans of action is now simple for me; the days of being engulfed in a fog of anxiety are long gone.

The Scientific Basis of Depression and Anxiety

Depression and anxiety have a long history in human history and were once necessary survival strategies. Like a prehistoric warning system, anxiety assisted our ancestors in identifying dangers in the natural world. It still acts as our internal safety net, alerting us to potential threats. When danger is detected, the brain's amygdala releases stress chemicals to get the body ready for "fight or flight." Although beneficial, anxiety can become excessively sensitive and result in recurring bouts of uneasiness (Walker Center, 2022).

Unlike typical mood swings, depression is a complicated emotional state characterized by biological imbalances. It results in persistent melancholy, pessimism, and disinterest. It descends upon us like a thick blanket of darkness, resulting from dysregulation of neurotransmitters such as dopamine and serotonin. Depression is influenced by both heredity and life experiences.

It is essential to comprehend these circumstances. Both have a neurological basis. Though protective, anxiety can become overwhelming. Depression modifies brain chemistry, resulting in depressed moods that last. It's critical to acknowledge depression as a real medical illness. Addressing these mental health issues requires compassion and awareness.

Common Signs of Depression and Anxiety

Think of your mind as a caffeine-hungry squirrel, full of racing ideas, unceasing concern, and a pervasive sense that something is going to go crazy. It's possible that your heart will become agitated and start beating like a jackhammer. The butterflies in your stomach, oh,! You seem to be hosting a party for anxiety!

The signs of anxiety

Anxiety can be compared to a large parade of "what ifs" marching past, a group of nerves having a party, and a lot of anxieties playing pranks. We're going to talk about the signs of anxiety, which may make even the most composed minds tremble and behave strangely.

Consider that you and I are at an amusement park, riding attractions like the extremely stressful Ferris wheel and the too-analytical merry-go-round. You have your imaginary popcorn with you. Who knows, you will win a stuffed animal at the whack-a-worry game.

● An excessive amount of worry is similar to having a worry button that is permanently in the "on" position. Do you ever have periods of time when you can't stop worrying about what might go wrong? Imagine that you felt that way about everything, even the little things, like putting on socks in the morning. It feels as though your mind has become an insatiable worry factory.

● Inattentiveness: Imagine this: Like a restless squirrel, you cannot seem to decide whether to burrow a hole or climb a tree. You may notice pacing like you are preparing for a marathon, shifting around in your chair, or tapping your foot. Calming? That is just a fancy name for anything you've heard about but still find difficult to understand. Staying seated? Unfortunately, your body missed that memo. It seems as though your relaxation mode is locked on snooze, and your energy level is turned up to eleven.

● Somatic Manifestations: Imagine your body involuntarily throwing an unexpected party. Your sweat glands decide it's time for an adventure at the water park, and your heart begins to race like it's trying out for a drumming performance. Your muscles may tense up like they are getting ready for a weightlifting competition, and your hands may tremble like they're training for a dance-off. It feels as though the "sweat and shake" setting on your body's thermostat is stuck.

● Hurrying ideas: Focus is difficult, like frenzied rabbits in a mental maze, since ideas race like running Olympians.

● Avoiding: Imagine being able to hit a magical "nope" button anytime you come across something that unnerves you. Therefore, you may react to situations that make you feel extremely anxious by responding, "Nope, not going there!" It is comparable to shielding your eyes from a terrifying movie scene in real life. The problem is that pressing more nope buttons will make your comfort zone smaller. Therefore, in your haste to avoid anxiety-inducing circumstances, you may unintentionally make your world smaller than a sweater in the dryer.

● Panic episodes: Has fear ever caused your body to organize a surprise party spontaneously? Your chest feels like it's throwing a small rave party, your breathing feels like you just finished a marathon, and your heart starts racing like it's attempting to win a sprint. Even though you're only waiting in line at the grocery store, your brain may even send out an emergency signal indicating the end of the world. It feels as though your body is pursuing you like a lion, even though all you did was pick up a milk carton. Greetings from the carnival of terror, where the adrenaline and a dash of "Oh no, what's happening?" fuel your body's roller-coaster journey.

IX. Management and Coping: Exposure therapy is used to help people with specific phobias become progressively less sensitive to the triggers they dread. Through this therapy, patients' anxiety reactions are lessened and their confidence is increased. Having the support of friends and family can also help in managing particular phobias.

It's critical to understand that certain phobias are treatable, and anyone exhibiting symptoms ought to consult a mental health expert for assistance. An individual's capacity to control their phobia, lessen avoidance behaviors, and live a more fulfilled life free from the ongoing fear and anxiety brought on by their particular trigger can significantly improve with early help.

5. Compulsive over-analyzing disorder (OCD)

OCD is a long-term, frequently crippling mental illness marked by intrusive, upsetting thoughts (called obsessions) and repetitive actions or ideas (called compulsions) carried out in an attempt to cope with the anxiety these obsessions generate. OCD can seriously impair a person's general wellbeing and cause major disruptions to everyday living.

Obsessive-Compulsive Disorder's salient characteristics include:

I. Obsessions: Recurrent intrusive, unpleasant, and upsetting thoughts, visions, or desires are known as obsessions. These ideas can cause severe discomfort or worry as they are frequently illogical. Fears of contamination, hurting oneself or others, or worrying about making a mistake are common obsessions.

II. Compulsions: People with OCD who experience compulsions are driven to engage in repetitive mental or behavioral activities as a result of their obsessions. Although they only offer momentary respite, these routines are meant to lessen the distress brought on by obsessions. Frequent compulsions include counting, praying, checking locks or appliances frequently, and compulsive hand washing.

III. Time-Consuming: OCD routines can impede day-to-day functioning and take a lot of time. Compulsions can cause OCD sufferers to spend hours every day engaging in them, which can interfere with daily routines, relationships, and employment.

IV. Distress: Compulsions frequently result in more distress even when they momentarily reduce worry. Even though OCD sufferers are aware that their compulsions and obsessions are unreasonable, they are helpless to put an end to them.

V. Avoidance: persons with OCD may steer clear of persons, places, or events that can set off obsessions or compulsions. Avoidance like this can hinder chances for advancement in one's career or personal life and result in social isolation.

When To Get Expert Assistance

If your sleep anxiety interferes with your everyday activities and does not go away with self-help techniques, you might want to see a doctor. They are able to evaluate your health, offer a precise diagnosis, and suggest suitable courses of action, such as counseling or medication if needed.

Sleep anxiety is a disturbing illness that makes it difficult for you to get a good night's sleep. causes, and coping mechanisms related with sleep anxiety.

Never forget that you may always get expert assistance if you find it difficult to manage your sleep anxiety on your own. Make your health a priority and take the required actions to get a good night's sleep that will revitalize you.

Optimistic Phrases for Sleep Disorders

I'm letting go of my anxieties and embracing restful sleep.

This affirmation helps you to release your cares and anxiety so that you can sleep well and peacefully.

2. I am in charge of my thoughts and decide to get a good night's sleep.

It is within your power to regulate your ideas.

3. With each breath I take, I'm getting closer to a restful, deep slumber.

This affirmation helps to calm your body and mind by making a connection between breathing and the falling asleep process.

4. I feel secure, at ease, and prepared to go to sleep.

This affirmation helps you relax and get ready for sleep by recognizing your safety.

5. I get a good night's sleep that gives me energy for the next day.

This affirmation supports the notion that going to sleep is a fresh start that gives you more energy for the following day rather than merely an end.

6. The darkness embraces me like a friend while I sleep soundly.

With the help of this affirmation, the night becomes a friend who helps you get a good night's sleep instead of something to be frightened.

7. I have faith in the cycle of alertness and sleep.

This affirmation urges you to have faith in your body's innate sleep-wake cycle.

8. I'm embracing the serenity of sleep and letting go of the stress of today.

With the use of this affirmation, you may let go of the stress from the day and be ready for a restful night's sleep.

9. My mind and body are in balance, prepared for a good night's sleep.

The balance between your body and mind is emphasized in this affirmation, which is essential for sound sleep.

10. Everything is peaceful, and I fall asleep.

This affirmation assists you in visualizing a calm setting that promotes restful sleep.

11. I am appreciative of sleep's healing properties.

This affirmation can improve your attitude toward sleep by fostering thankfulness for the healing function of sleep.

12. I am in charge, so my anxieties cannot keep me up at night.

The idea that your thoughts, not your problems, are what control this assertion reinforces you.

13. I enjoy sleep since it's a healthy, natural component of life.

This affirmation lessens any sleep-related tension by promoting the idea that it is a necessary and beneficial aspect of life.

- **Effective Symptom Reduction:** Several studies have demonstrated that cognitive behavioral therapy (CBT) is very successful in easing the symptoms of depression and anxiety. It offers sustained comfort.

- **Improved Coping Skills:** CBT gives you the tools you need to deal with stress, difficult circumstances, and emotional triggers.

Prevention of Relapse: By addressing the underlying thought patterns that contribute to anxiety and depression, cognitive behavioral therapy (CBT) can help prevent these disorders from reoccurring.

Your Own CBT Resource Kit:

Although consulting with a certified CBT therapist can be very helpful, self-help methods can also help you apply CBT concepts to your life. This is a condensed DIY CBT toolkit:

1. **Thought Journaling:** Write down any involuntary negative ideas you have in a journal. Once patterns have been identified, attempt to refute and challenge them.

2. **Mindfulness Integration:** To improve your self-awareness and emotional control, incorporate mindfulness techniques into your CBT journey.

Behavioral Experiments: Try out novel behaviors that contradict your ingrained mental habits. Begin with modest, doable measures.

Positive Affirmations: Make up and recite uplifting affirmations to offset self-defeating thoughts. Make use of these as reminders of your value and potential.

The Path to Expert Assistance:

Even while self-help CBT methods have their uses, there might be occasions when seeking the advice of a qualified CBT therapist is beneficial. They can offer you specialized advice, insights, and methods that are catered to your particular problems.

Recall that CBT focuses on creating better thought patterns and coping skills rather than on rejecting or suppressing emotions. Discovering the benefits of cognitive behavioral therapy (CBT) can help you change the way you think, lessen the effects of anxiety and depression, and take back control of your mental and emotional health.

3. Physical Symptoms: Trembling, blushing, perspiration, a fast heartbeat, and stomach discomfort are examples of physical symptoms of social anxiety. The child's anxiety in social circumstances may worsen due to these physical reactions.

4. Negative Self-Perception: Kids who struggle with social anxiety frequently have a poor opinion of themselves. Their anxiety may be worsened by their perception that they are unworthy, unlikable, or inept in social situations.

5. Interference with Daily Life: If social anxiety is not handled, it can hinder a child's capacity to succeed academically, form friendships, and acquire critical life

skills. It may have a lasting impact on their confidence and sense of self.

3.

14. Make your directions to your kids simpler.

Prolonged lectures frequently fail to produce the intended effects. Try reducing your request to a single word or phrase rather than bugging or griping about a task or chore. In this manner, your child will comprehend the lesson without experiencing guilt or overwhelm.

For example, rather than stating, "You were supposed to clean the litter box yesterday, and it's still not done," you may add, "Dianna, the cat!"

Rather than saying, "I told you to pack your bags 10 minutes ago," you may say, "Kids, backpacks!"

15. Give your child a variety of options to choose from.

Certain kids may not receive strict instructions well. Rather, make a chore or directive into a fun "this or that" situation. When your child feels like they have some influence over their daily routine and decisions, they are more inclined to cooperate.

Instead of telling your child to bring their own lunch, you might ask them if they would rather have ham and cheese or a peanut butter and jelly sandwich.

Give your kids a few options for what to wear each day rather than just telling them to get ready.

It's acceptable when there aren't always acceptable alternatives available. Just offer options when it's feasible.

Significant Achievers and Changes

It's important to examine the significant changes and influences that have molded CBT's development into the complex therapeutic method we know today after highlighting the early pioneers, such as Albert Ellis and Aaron T. Beck.

As actual data supporting CBT's effectiveness started accumulating in the 1980s and 1990s, other pioneers such as Donald Meichenbaum presented the idea of "cognitive restructuring," a technique that focused on changing maladaptive thought processes. This huge breakthrough underscored the need for active, systematic change in one's cognitive processes rather than just being aware of them.

Mindfulness-Based Cognitive Therapy (MBCT), created by Zindel Segal, Mark Williams, and John Teasdale, was another revolutionary development. By combining mindfulness techniques with conventional CBT techniques, people were able to recognize their thoughts and feelings without necessarily attempting to alter or get rid of them. By assisting people in becoming more cognizant of their thought patterns and establishing a buffer between thought and emotion, the goal was to break the cycle of depressed relapse.

The field of CBT was further expanded by Marsha Linehan's introduction of Dialectical Behavior Therapy (DBT) in the late 1980s. Originally developed to address Borderline Personality Disorder, DBT integrates mindfulness practices with cognitive-behavioral methods to promote acceptance and change. This dual acceptance-change axis provided a sophisticated method that was especially helpful for efficient interpersonal communication and emotional control.

These significant contributors also changed the way CBT is used. The original session format, which included average 12 to 16 weeks of therapy, started to change. Shorter, more intense sessions were being investigated in some circumstances, particularly with the introduction of internet-based CBT. Furthermore, more specialized interventions that catered to particular diseases like obsessive-compulsive disorder (OCD), post-traumatic stress disorder (PTSD), and even eating disorders have supplanted the earlier one-size-fits-all approach.

Incorporating cultural sensitivity into CBT methods was another significant change. Therapists increasingly grasped how much cultural influences impact emotional and cognitive processes. Because of this, CBT models that have been culturally adjusted have been created, acknowledging the impact of an individual's social, racial, and religious backgrounds on their experience.

Technology has a role that cannot be disregarded either. With the development of digital platforms and mobile applications, CBT approaches are now more widely accessible and effective, allowing more people to take advantage of these beneficial psychological therapies.

CBT did more than merely alter; it broadened its scope, adjusted to societal shifts, and included complementary methods. These changes were not accidental; rather, they were the result of motivated academics,, empirically validated, and culturally sensitive type of psychotherapy.

As we get further into this book, you'll see that these key players and changes directly contribute to the complexity and depth of CBT. By incorporating additional levels of adaptability and applicability, they have enhanced the therapy's framework, transforming CBT into a highly successful and globally applicable therapeutic paradigm.

Exercise 2: Indirect Effects

So that we can subsequently concentrate on the present, let's begin by addressing the past. To know how to handle present issues, you must be conscious of your past stressful experiences and how you have evolved over time. Focus first on your feelings. Please make a list of them, attempt to recall the first time you experienced them in the past, and remember what transpired. You don't have to recall your first angry moment as a toddler because nobody could remember it. You can, however, remember an instance when you were extremely irate and did something that is still ingrained in your memory. Perhaps you were upset because you were disappointed in one of your friends' actions, or perhaps it was your first argument with your parents and you yelled at them.

This practice facilitates the relationship between emotions and their triggering events. It also assists you in becoming conscious of how you now respond to similar feelings. If you were to quarrel with your parents again, would your response be the same as it was the first time? Most likely not. Realizing all of the advancements you have made in recent years and adopting a more upbeat outlook on the improvements you can yet make can be achieved by thinking back on your past. You must reflect on negative and positive feelings to fully finish the exercise and become aware of both. Actually, every emotion is necessary for your own growth.

Exercise 3: A Retrospective Walk

Making a life timeline is a helpful practice that can assist you in understanding which historical events shaped your life. It's possible that you were aware of it but believed it to be a silly pastime. You could have assured yourself that you would not have attempted anything like that. Try it at least once in your lifetime.

All you need is a pen and a piece of paper. All you have to do is draw a line; it only matters if it's precisely straight. Drawing ability is not required. Your birth is undoubtedly the most significant event in your life and the point at which everything began, so write it at the left end of the line. Add all the events that you believe arc significant after that.

Remember that there may be significant life changes, such as relocating to a new place or having your first conversation with your best friend of the present. However, they can also be quite little, like the time you had a great time with your friends or when one of your instructors said something really nice to you.

Take as much time as necessary to do the task, and then review all of the things you recorded. The things that stick in your memory and the information that you value higher may surprise you. In this manner, you become aware of the things you hold dear and the unpleasant experiences you can't seem to forget.

Stress And Time Management

Consider time management to be your stress-reduction secret. It is similar to possessing a superpower that makes you feel less anxious and helps you maintain control. We'll cover three key strategies in this part to help you make the most of this superpower:

1. Planning and Setting Priorities

Let's say you have a large plate of food that you are still working on at a time. You begin with the tastiest portions first, correct? That's the main purpose of priority. It entails prioritizing your most crucial tasks and completing them first.

Example: Suppose you are balancing your family, job, and household tasks. You create a plan rather than attempting to complete everything at once. You determine that spending time with your family and completing a job project are the two most important things to do today. Housework can wait. You will feel more in control and experience less stress in this way.

2. Making sensible objectives

Have you ever dropped a bag of groceries because you were trying to carry too many at once? That occurs when you have too many or too many goals. It could make you feel stressed out and overburdened. Realistic goal-setting involves dividing difficult activities into smaller, more doable chunks.

As an illustration, suppose you wish to pick up a new talent. You break it down rather than attempting to master it all at once. Every day, you gain a little knowledge. You'll experience less tension and a sense of satisfaction as you reach these little objectives.

3. Saying No and Assigning

Consider that the amount of items you can fit in your backpack is limited. Attempting to carry too much makes it tiresome and cumbersome. Saying no is about taking on only what you can manage, and delegation is about spreading the workload.

Example: Since you're already busy, you decline the invitation to join another committee at work. You say no rather than accepting and being overburdened. You also understand that you can ask your family for assistance if you need it instead of doing everything at home. You'll experience less tension and hardship in this method.

Hence, time management involves prioritizing key tasks, dividing large jobs into smaller ones, and refraining from trying to complete everything by oneself. It's similar to possessing a superpower that can reduce stress and make your life happier and easier.

The Avoidance Cycle

Social anxiety is well known for its ability to repeat itself in an unbreakable loop. Avoidance is a common coping strategy used in response to social anxiety; it provides a little reprieve from worry but, paradoxically, makes it worse over time. Avoiding social situations can be relieving lost chances, untapped potential, and a growing sense of loneliness.

Breaking Free: The Path to Knowledge

In order to overcome social anxiety, one must go on a deep introspective and comprehending journey. This journey necessitates removing the outer layers of anxiety and self-doubt and reaching the very center of one's insecurities. It requires facing past traumas, overcoming skewed cognitive habits, and becoming an expert at redefining one's own self-perception.

Nonetheless, comprehending social anxiety is a collaborative effort. Empathy is required from oneself as well as from the community around us. Breaking the bonds of prejudice and fostering an atmosphere of acceptance and compassion requires teamwork.

A Sneak Peek at What's in Store

In the upcoming chapters, we shall explore the complex world of social anxiety in further detail. We will scrutinize its origins, study its numerous forms, and, most crucially, empower you with a comprehensive arsenal of methods and skills to break free from its vice-like hold. Social anxiety may be a difficult enemy, but armed with understanding as our guiding light, we can embark on a transforming path toward a more confident, connected, and fulfilled self. Our investigation promises to uncover the deep nuances of this emotional tapestry, bringing clarity to the complex subject of social anxiety, and exposing the route to recovery and self-discovery.

- Self-Compassion: Extend to yourself the same care and understanding that you offer to a cherished friend. Self-compassion entails acknowledging that everyone meets hurdles and makes mistakes. Embracing self-compassion mitigates self-criticism and bolsters emotional resiliency.

- Setting Realistic Expectations: Often, self-imposed expectations contribute to social anxiety and stress. Learning to develop reachable, realistic goals lessens self-imposed strain.

- Learning from Experience: Embrace mistakes and failures as stepping stones to growth. Instead of obsessing on them as sources of concern, embrace them as chances for personal development.

- Seeking Professional treatment: Should social anxiety and stress persist and adversely influence your life, ongoing professional treatment is vital. Therapists give information, coping skills, and support suited to your particular circumstances.

Let's investigate the incredible benefits that mindful eating can bring for anxiety management:

Release tension and anxiety: During times of stress or worry, we often find ourselves turning to mindless eating as a short escape. However, by embracing mindful eating, we discover the potential of slowing down and immersing ourselves in the present moment. This increase in awareness can lead us to make healthier dietary choices, fostering a more pleasant relationship with sustenance.

Nurture digestion: Anxiety may wreak havoc on our digestive system, causing discomfort and misery. Through mindful eating, we create an environment of calm, reducing tension and helping our bodies to absorb food more properly. The act of tasting each bite consciously enables us to tune in to our body's requirements, facilitating greater absorption of nutrients and relieving digestive discomfort.

Cultivate good weight management: Mindful eating helps us to be more responsive to our hunger and fullness cues. By paying attention to these signals, we can prevent overeating and make decisions that honor our body's demands. This thoughtful approach to feeding supports healthy weight management and fosters a good body image.

Deepen self-awareness: Through the practice of mindful eating, we begin on a path of self-discovery. We develop a profound grasp of how our emotions affect our eating patterns. By fostering mindfulness in our eating choices,

In conclusion, practicing mindful eating is vital in reducing anxiety and fostering our general well-being. By immersing ourselves fully in the act of eating, we alleviate tension and anxiety, boost digestion, promote healthy weight control, and deepen our self-awareness.

By conversing honestly with your spouse, reservations that can beget solicitude are removed, leaving space for a healthy appreciation of the connection.

Enjoy the Present When you notice your studies beginning to guess about the fortune of your partnership in times to come, it's normally wise to nip it in the club and appreciate the current moment. Considering whether or not your lover will truly remain in your life five times, or whether they'll still find you appealing in months to come, merely takes down from cherishing your present joy. rather, it burdens you with concern about unborn conditions that may not indeed materialize. To calm your concerns, appreciate your present reality, and taste the happiness of being with a person you have chosen and who has also chosen to be with you at the time.Confront Your Anxiety It may appear strange to embrace your worries while striving to get over them, yet this is one of the most effective techniques to bring your feelings under control.Are you nervous because of a previous unsuccessful relationship? Maybe you worry about not being good enough for love because you struggle with how you perceive yourself. Questioning the causes for your anxiety in connections could help you comprehend these issues and tackle them correctly. Attend remedy In some circumstances, carrying professional backup to manage your anxiety may be the finest choice for bringing it under control.

Through remedy, you may get the crucial counsel to modify negative and dysfunctional thoughts about yourself, your tone- worth, and your station towards your partnership. treatment may also provide ideal techniques to regulate your anxiousness to avoid endless injury to the partnership. How to Ease Anxiety at Night Experiencing anxiety as you lay down to sleep at night could emerge due to stress, an anxiety ailment, or other health enterprises.

Treatment options can include pharmaceutical, life, or remedy-based approaches, depending on the cause.

Anxiety is a deadly emotion that begins with feelings of concern and anxiety. When pressure persists for an extended length of time, often without apparent cause, anxiety sets in.

Stressful situations, like a first date or a job interview, might make you feel upset.

However, if this feeling of dread doesn't go away and actually keeps you awake at night, you might be suffering from anxiety. Please continue reading to learn the likely causes of your nighttime worry and how to deal with it.

Why is it happening at night? Your day — and late life — can be disrupted by anxiety. Research Trusted Source reveals sleep loss may induce anxiety. Research also demonstrates that the liability of poor sleep is a higher-trusted source among persons suffering from interior health issues, including anxiousness. Because of this, managing your sleep disorders and addressing your nighttime anxiety are both essential steps in improving your quality of life. Signs of anxiety can be bright and varied. Anxiety affects everyone else. Symptoms could appear any time of day, early in the morning, or late at night. Common Trusted Source indicators of anxiety include emotions of apprehensiveness, uneasiness, or worry, trouble concentrating, trouble going to sleep or staying asleep, and gastrointestinal issues. A fear attack is another symptom that an anxious person may experience.

Establishing objectives: Following the assessment, the therapist works with the couple to create specific goals for their therapy. These goals may include improving communication, understanding the impact of ADHD, and developing more adept problem-solving techniques. The therapy process has direction when precise goals are set.

Meetings and methods: After that, couples attend routine therapy sessions where they go through a range of problem-solving techniques and activities. In order to enhance the application of the concepts discussed in therapy, these sessions may involve role-playing, communication drills, or even homework assignments.

Suggestions and modifications:

In order to assess the effectiveness of the tactics employed, the therapist asks the couple for feedback as the session progresses. The therapist may modify or adjust the plan in light of this feedback in order to better suit the goals and needs of the couple.

The role of the therapist:

The therapist serves as both a guide and a facilitator in couples therapy. Thanks to their education and experience, they are able to navigate the challenges faced by relationships impacted by ADHD and offer answers.

Creating a Secure Area

The therapist must create a safe, accepting space In order to foster open communication and develop trust in the therapeutic alliance, this environment is crucial.

Providing Ordered Guidance:

Therapists teach couples strategies and techniques to manage the impact of ADHD on their relationship.

As part of this counseling, effective communication strategies, conflict resolution techniques, and stress management techniques are typically taught.

Therapists encourage full participation from both partners to guarantee that the viewpoints of each partner are heard. They encourage dialogue, ask pointed questions, and provide insights to enhance understanding and resolution.

Monitoring Development: Throughout the course of therapy, therapists monitor the couple's progress towards their planned goals. They address problems, provide feedback, and modify the treatment plan as needed to ensure the couple gets the best outcomes.

Typical Symptoms

Let's examine some typical signs of nervousness. These symptoms can take many different forms, and they frequently change based on the kind and severity of the anxiety illness. It is essential to comprehend these signs in order to identify anxiety disorders early and treat them effectively.

Excessive Worry: One of the main indicators of many anxiety disorders, including Generalised Anxiety Disorder (GAD), is excessive and uncontrollable worry. Even when there is little or no cause for concern, people with GAD frequently worry excessively about commonplace issues like relationships, money, or health.

Restlessness and Agitation: People who are anxious frequently have restless and agitated feelings. They could find it difficult to remain motionless, pace, or move their limbs incessantly. This physical sign of restlessness is the elevated arousal linked to anxiousness.

Tension in the Muscles: Often, anxiety results in tense muscles. Individuals who are anxious may feel tightness, stiffness, or even pain in their muscles, usually in the back, shoulders, or neck.

Fast Heartbeat: One of the most prevalent physical signs of worry is tachycardia, or an elevated heart rate. Even in the absence of physical activity, palpitations or a racing heart sensation may accompany it.

Breathlessness: Breathing difficulties or a sensation of being out of breath are frequently reported by those who are anxious. This is frequently the result of quick, shallow breathing patterns. Because this symptom resembles the physical symptoms of a panic attack, it may cause more concern.

perspiration: Anxiety often triggers profuse perspiration, particularly in the forehead, underarms, and palms. In social or stressful circumstances, it can be very apparent.

Trembling or Shaking: Involuntary trembling or shaking, usually in the hands or legs, can be brought on by anxiety. This shaking is a reaction to the production of stress hormones and is associated with the body's increased level of awareness.

Nausea or Stomach Discomfort: When feeling worried, a lot of people may suffer from nausea, upset stomachs, or even diarrhoea. This is a symptom where the gut-brain link is important.

These are the methods that CBT can teach you. These are methods that you can independently learn and apply to yourself. But receiving CBT from a therapist or other mental health specialist can also be beneficial. In the event that you decide to receive CBT from a mental health expert, you will often go through four stages:

The assessment phase is the initial meeting between your therapist and yourself. Typically, this happens during the first several sessions. The therapist will be able to diagnose you, determine the length of your treatment, and evaluate your mental health based on the basic information you offer. Take some time to list the distressing circumstances you have encountered in your life thus far. For instance, a medical condition, divorce, rage, or grief. After that, you could work with your therapist to explore each of these concerns in order to identify which is most impacting you.

Cognitive stage: During this phase, you and your therapist collaborate to examine and comprehend your ideas. This could involve talking about previous experiences that have influenced your way of thinking or important people who have had an impact on you. You will become conscious of your feelings, ideas, and convictions about who you are, where you've come from, and what's around you via self-examination and contemplation. You'll get more understanding of how you view specific previous events, how you understand particular behaviours, and how you view your own personality and value. You can only determine which of your thoughts and beliefs are false or unfavorable by outlining them. You can also recognize which of your negative ideas are causing your problems. Once you have identified the specific concerns, you will divide your challenges into manageable chunks (you can accomplish this by journaling your ideas and patterns of behavior). After that, you and your therapist will examine your feelings, behaviors, and ideas to see if they are healthy or realistic. You will examine how your feelings and ideas impact you and one another.

The phase of behavior: During this phase, you and your therapist collaborate to develop new thought patterns, which you then start using in your daily life to develop better and more beneficial behaviors and habits. You'll start to reframe your false and pessimistic ideas as you develop the ability to distinguish between facts and feelings. You'll put certain adjustments into practice on a daily basis. These adjustments could involve confronting distressing ideas as they arise and substituting them with more positive and healthful ones, or identifying when you're going to act in a way that would exacerbate your emotional state or circumstance and acting instead in a way that will benefit you. Between sessions, you can receive homework to help you hone these abilities and develop constructive thought patterns. You will then report to your therapist at the end of each session how you implemented those adjustments and your experiences doing so. Your therapist will be better positioned to provide additional suggestions after considering this.

Learning stage: In order to make sure that the improvements you've made thus far are long-lasting and durable, you will collaborate with your therapist during this phase. You'll pick up strategies for handling or avoiding relapses.

Platforms for Mobile Mental Health Assessments

Comprehensive self-assessment tools for anxiety are available on integrated platforms for mental health testing. These tools include the following: Numerous Assessments: These platforms give users access to a wide range of assessments, including stress questionnaires, cognitive assessments, and anxiety symptom scales. Users can select the tests that most closely match their own needs.

Data Integration: A single user profile may contain data gathered from several self-evaluation tools. The holistic approach provides this all-encompassing viewpoint on a person's possible mental health condition. Customised recommendations: Based on the results of self-assessments, these platforms frequently generate customised recommendations for self-help strategies, treatment options, or get in touch with mental health professionals.

Uses for Meditation and Mindfulness

Self-assessment apps that teach meditation and mindfulness are becoming more and more used as anxiety therapy tools:

Being aware Self-Evaluation: A lot of these apps have self-evaluation features that let users assess their level of awareness in the here and now. Over time, users can track their own progress in developing greater attention.

Sessions of Guided Meditation and Breathwork: Vital elements of mindfulness applications are both guided meditation sessions and breathing exercises. Users can assess how much they have relaxed and de-stressed after using these approaches by reflecting on themselves.

Monitoring One's success: A lot of mindfulness apps come with tools for monitoring one's success that let users log how often and how long they meditate. These numbers may help us understand how consistent their mindfulness practice is.

Communities and Forums Providing Assistance and Support Online Communities and forums providing assistance and support, although not conventional self-assessment techniques, are essential to the self-diagnosis and management of anxiety:

Peer support is the ability for people to connect with others who have similar experiences and problems related to anxiety. People may become more adept at identifying their own worry patterns by exchanging stories, concepts, and coping mechanisms with one another. Self-Revelation via Anonymity Many online forums offer a safe space where people can express themselves anonymously. Users are able to openly and honestly communicate their anxiety symptoms, triggers, and concerns without fear of judgment. Exchange of Knowledge: Online forum users frequently contribute self-assessment methods, strategies, and resources that they have found useful in their own journeys towards anxiety management. Technology advancements and psychological research have led to a significant evolution in anxiety treatments and self-assessment tools in recent years. With the ability to identify anxiety symptoms, triggers, and cognitive patterns, these tools enable users to make more informed decisions regarding self-care strategies, alternate forms of treatment, and, when required, seeking professional assistance.

Simplifying Your Life To Streamline Your Lifestyle For Mental Clarity

The reason for brain fog dictates the course of treatment. Lifestyle modifications can also be beneficial.

A. Reduce the amount of time you spend on the phone and computer, and remember to take pauses.

B. Think positively to ease tension.

C. Change what you eat

D. Get seven to eight hours of sleep every day, and make sure you go to bed by 10 p.m.

E. Engage in regular exercise

F. Steer clear of coffee, cigarettes, and alcoholic beverages in the afternoon.

G. Finding pleasurable pursuits

Ten: Fostering Inner Peace and Quietness; Taking Care of a Quiet and Peaceful Mind kind and helpful. All you have to do is find out how.

What is inner peace exactly?

A state of serenity in which you feel comfortable around people, yourself, and your environment is known as inner peace. It's about being comfortable and totally present in your own skin. Stress, worry, and anxiety have less of an impact.

You accept everything that makes you uniquely you—your interests, your goals, and your imperfections—when you are at peace with yourself. Additionally, you experience less worry, anxiety, and tension because you are more tolerant of the circumstances and the world around you.

At its core, actionable equanimity is inner calm.

What is equanimity exactly?

It takes more than just taking quick stress breaks or moments of relaxation to achieve inner calm. You might be able to maintain your inner peace by remaining calm. You can cultivate the skill of equanimity, which will enable you to remain composed and in control of your emotions no matter what challenges life presents. In other words, you're okay if everything is OK, but you're also okay if it's not.

Being mindful is crucial.

There is no wish that can bring about inner peace. It is an expression of who you are, what you do, and what you create.

Suggestions for using mindfulness to achieve inner peace

1. Make meditation a habit:

Even though it's a simple practice, meditation can significantly improve your mental health. It encourages composure and a more profound sense of peace.

You meditate in what way? Locate a peaceful area far from the throng. Shut your eyes, inhale deeply, then release the breath slowly. It doesn't matter if you finish everything precisely; a few minutes might go a long way. Recall that you have access to tools such as Calm to help you. To assist you in beginning a meditation practice, we offer hundreds of meditations and activities.

2. Stay in the present:

How often do you find yourself dwelling on the past or worrying about what might happen in the future? You most likely do if you're anything like the rest of us. But as you know, we really only have the present moment. Live it and accept it. Life exists in the here and now.

How can you make the most of the here and now? Make an effort to fully commit to everyday activities like eating, walking, or even doing chores. Observe the sensations of sound, smell, and sight around you. Inner peace is the outcome, which is similar to giving your brain a little vacation.

Anxiety Disorders: What Are They?

People with anxiety disorders are those who experience extreme dread and anxiety for real or imagined reasons. Since the turn of the 20th century, when it was discovered that anxiety and dread might damage a person's ability to perform both mental and physical tasks, it has been classified as a psychiatric science. It shows up as a number of illnesses that fall under the umbrella of panic attacks, physical stress, and mental anxiety. Many times, anxiety persists even after the perceived threat or object of fear has vanished.

In response to the question, "What are anxiety disorders?" it would be helpful to identify the symptoms as well. It is not uncommon for someone to feel actual pain and terror, which may continue for a few minutes to several hours. Other common symptoms include nausea, dizziness, trouble breathing, and shivering. Phobia is defined by fear of situations, objects, people, or animals. It is considered a subtype of anxiety disorder. This is typically brought on by a negative encounter with a thing, situation, or animal that you fear. For instance, a negative snake-related experience could be the cause of a snake phobia. Another category of anxiety condition is obsession. Excessive feelings of attachment to people, things, or circumstances can set off an odd mental illness that transforms a strong fixation into compulsive actions. Anxiety related to separation is another related anxiety. When a person becomes estranged from a loved one, an excessive amount of connection to them may cause them to lose control. In this case, if an affectionate feeling is felt deeply for the person, it becomes abnormal. The actions of the person in question become irrational when the beloved is alone. Trauma results in detachment findings, and this causes excruciating agony.

The classic example of an anxiety disorder is when a person has persistent terror for hours or days at a time when they are presented with a constant danger or chance of illness or ruin from their job or organisation. These kinds of episodes are better identified and classified as panic attacks. Anxiety attacks cause physical symptoms, including uneasiness, shortness of breath, and an accelerated heartbeat in the person experiencing them. This is because the emotional condition of the person begins to affect the physical state. It can occasionally take up to six months for anxiety to develop into a chronic condition.

Children with anxiety disorders may also experience abnormalities in the way they learn and interact with others when they are plagued by ongoing worries. They experience mental despair, cognitive decline, and total failure in academic pursuits. Even their physical health is affected because the majority of affected youngsters have dysfunctions including dyspepsia, upset stomachs, elevated blood pressure and heart rates, nausea, shortness of breath, and several other illnesses. Many will eventually experience problems sleeping, which will only make things worse. youngsters are also affected by separation anxiety, and the most severe cases of this kind of anxiety are those that include youngsters.

It is crucial that children's minor worries do not develop into anxiety disorders. Healthy family dynamics aid in preventing such incidents. However, it is always a good idea to receive competent advice and give therapy for these conditions in case the inevitable happens. The best course of action in cases when the observed symptoms indicate that the children's anxieties are consistent with anxiety disorders is psychotherapy.

Time for a joyous conclusion

For more than two decades, Michele has been employed by the same company. His previous role was entry-level, but now he was in management. He was passionate about the work he did and loved what he accomplished. But the rigors of the work had worn him down over the years. He oversaw a group of workers, routinely put in long hours, and dealt with challenging clients. Despite experiencing months of stress and anxiety, he persisted, believing it was only a temporary state.

Michele finally had enough one day. There was a noticeable sense of tension in the room as he met with a challenging client. Michele had dedicated months of his life to this project and worked tirelessly on it. Nevertheless, the client proved to be challenging and demanding, and they were not happy with the work. Despite his best efforts to stay composed and professional, Michele could feel his stress level rising.

Michele blew up when the stress reached its peak. He stormed out of the meeting and quit his job immediately. Walking out of the building, he experienced a wave of relief. He felt free for the first time in years.

Michele took some time off to reflect on his life and his future goals. He came to the realization that he had been ignoring his physical and emotional health for years and that something had to change. He enrolls in classes in order to broaden his skill set and consider employment options. He began eating well and exercising frequently. He rekindled his passion for music while spending time with his loved ones.

Michele began to feel better when he began to take care of himself. He came to the realization that he needed to alter because he had been living his life automatically. He started looking at different employment options and eventually discovered a position he loved. He began working for a nonprofit that provided aid to those in need. He knew that he had made the proper choice, and he felt happy and fulfilled.

Through experience, Michele has learned that burnout is not always a bad thing. It might serve as a wake-up call that compels you to take stock of your life and make adjustments. You can use burnout as a chance for pleasure and personal development if you look after yourself and consider new work options.

Typical Anxiety Symptoms and Signs

Although worry is a common and healthy human emotion, anxiety disorders can develop when excessive or persistent anxiety occurs. Understanding the typical indications and manifestations of anxiety is essential for prompt assistance and intervention. We'll go into more detail about various manifestations here.

1. Excessive Worry: Persistent, excessive worry about a variety of life elements, such as relationships, employment, personal health, and the future, is one of

the main indicators of anxiety. This concern frequently exceeds what is reasonable given the circumstances.

2. Physical restlessness: People who are anxious may exhibit physical restlessness, which is frequently manifested as a pacing, fidgeting, or reluctance to relax. This agitation may be a physical manifestation of internal conflict.

3. Tension in the Muscles: Anxiety can cause physical discomfort and tension in the muscles. People may experience headaches from tension, aches and pains all over their bodies, or stiffness in their muscles.

4. Racing Thoughts: Racing or bothersome thoughts are a common side effect of anxiety. People may struggle to concentrate or de-stress because of an incessant flow of fears and hypothetical situations.

5. Elevated Heart Rate: Anxiety causes the body to react physiologically with an

increased heart rate. Even in non-stressful situations, people may have palpitations or a racing heartbeat.

6. Excessive Sweating and shaking: These physical symptoms of worry might include excessive sweating and shaking, especially in the hands. These sensations frequently appear in situations that make you feel anxious.

7. Symptoms related to the digestive system: Anxiety can have an impact on the digestive system, resulting in symptoms such as diarrhea, stomachaches, nausea, or irritable bowel syndrome (IBS).

8. Sleep Disturbances: Anxiety can interfere with sleep cycles, making it harder to go asleep, stay asleep, or get restorative sleep. Dreams that are vivid and terrifying are also typical.

9. Avoidance Behaviour: To avoid events or triggers that make them anxious, some people with anxiety may engage in avoidance behaviors. This avoidance can

cause problems in day-to-day living and support the persistence of worry.

10. irritation: Anxiety frequently leads to irritation or a snappy disposition. People might easily get angry or lash out at other people, especially when they're feeling stressed.

11. Cognitive Symptoms: Anxiety can affect one's ability to think clearly, making it harder to focus, remember things, or make decisions. People might start to lose their memories or have trouble thinking straight.

In order to determine the participants' awareness of the true purpose of the study, the researchers proceeded to ask more detailed questions about the subliminal pictures they had seen as the study reached its final segment.

Surprisingly, the findings supported the hypothesis that people are impacted by their innate emotional reactions to stimuli. According to the study's findings, participants who exclusively saw the photos intended to arouse disgust ended up utilizing more terms related to disgust in the word-completion portion. Additionally, these people were more likely to use derogatory language to express their emotions, and the majority of them selected the "scary movie test."

The same outcomes ultimately occurred for those who saw only the images that made them feel afraid; they were also more likely to select terms associated with fear, and the majority of them chose the "strange food test" over the "scary movie test."

The study's conclusions turned out to be some of the first proof that certain emotions can actually be triggered without the subject even realizing it. Furthermore, even though the study did not genuinely look into how people become aware of their feelings, the researcher did develop a further theory. According to the study, people eventually become aware of the emotion they are experiencing when their sentiments reach a full-blown stage because that is when they are able to recognize their own behaviors and responses. However, when someone's emotions are weak, they are more likely to be weakly tied to their emotions, making it more difficult for them to notice the reactions and behaviours.

Motivation and Emotions

Generally speaking, emotions and motivation are considered to be two entirely distinct physiological traits with a seemingly cause-and-effect relationship. It's not always clear, though, how strong their relationship truly is.

Motivation plays a crucial role in an individual's emotions as it aids in making decisions about acting on feelings. For example, when a human comes across a wild animal that appears protective, their immediate anxicty and desire to avoid harm will drive them to try to move away from the risky circumstance.

Motivation can be described as an individual's readiness to do the necessary effort to accomplish a particular objective. The self-regulatory theory of motivation is based on the notion that people care about their ability to change in order to achieve a goal.

Most of the time, motivation is thought of as a tool that encourages someone to act or behave in a particular way in order to accomplish a goal. On the other hand, emotions are thought of as the feelings that manifest due to the underlying motivation. In actuality, though, the connection between motivation and emotion is far more nuanced.

The majority of psychologists believe that there are three main reasons why emotions and motivation interact. The first explanation is that a person's behavior activates or energizes feelings and impulses that are aroused. Emotions and motives just naturally go together, which is the second explanation for the pair's relationship. The fact that even the most fundamental emotions frequently possess motivating qualities is the third and last explanation for why the two are seen to be related. For instance, someone is more likely to be driven to do well that day when they are feeling happy. More precisely, someone who is feeling upbeat will probably be more driven to prepare for an impending test. A person may find it harder to concentrate when they are feeling depressed, which makes them feel less inclined to study.

The less obvious relationship between motivation and emotions is that both are related to energy or intensity instead of just direction or information. This implies that motivation and feelings are more influenced by the experience than by the actual content being used. With regard to the exam study example, the person's motivation and feelings have been more concentrated on the drive to finish the study than on the content of the material being studied.

The fact that pressure and heat are frequently associated with motivation and emotion is another similarity between the two. On the other hand, cognition is more closely related to "coldness." It's also important to note that motivation and emotions are influenced by an individual's relationship with themselves, with others, and with their surroundings.

A new degree of understanding is emerging among many theories on the relationship between motivation and emotions. Theorists can even explain how emotions and motivation are linked to the point where people act in specific ways in the hopes of feeling happy and experiencing other positive emotions. Keeping that in mind, it has become increasingly clear that feelings can be viewed as one of the benefits or drawbacks associated with engaging in certain behavior that is driven by the prospect of happiness in the future.

How to Learn to Listen Well

Ineffective communicators believe that "listening" is just waiting for their opportunity to speak while planning their answer in their head. This is a serious error. There is so much more to listening than meets the eye; it's an opportunity to give someone else a voice, foster emotional connection, and demonstrate empathy.

We're going to cover the fundamentals of effective listening today, followed by an exercise that will help you put these ideas into practice.

While it is important in and of itself, listening is more than just providing someone the opportunity to say what's on their mind. Additionally, the first step towards personal improvement is listening.

Knowing that the other person is paying attention to you at that level makes you feel important. You feel needed, secure, and understood as a result. To be heard is to be validated.

Now consider a situation where you felt you had something important to say but were not given that kind of attention. The other person did not acknowledge your statements because they were preoccupied, staring at their phone, obviously thinking about something else, or mentally preparing their answer.

You were made to feel small, unimportant, and unnoticed.

It felt like a slap in the face when they refused or were unable to listen to you.

Regretfully, the skill of attentive listening is vanishing faster than one may think. Our principal means of communication are no longer face-to-face interactions or even phone calls.

What Makes Someone a Good Listener

Improved relationships in both personal and professional spheres are possible due to people's preference for listeners; better problem solving for both themselves and others; learning diverse perspectives to expand one's horizons; retention of important information crucial to personal and professional success; ease of decision making due to increased availability of information; avoidance of conflicts and misunderstandings as a result of attentive listening; and increased confidence as a result of having access to information and the ability to share it with others.

Practise breathing techniques.

Breathing deeply is something else you should do. As much oxygen as you can should be consumed both before and during the interview. You should be breathing heavily since it will make you feel better. Furthermore, if you can only concentrate on one thing, it should be proper breathing. You should observe a simple meltdown of your nerves when you do this.

Be upbeat.

Have faith that the place you're heading is where you belong and are intended to be. Being confident is important, and if you project a positive and upbeat attitude, you'll come prepared to prove your knowledge throughout the interview. The most crucial thing is to persevere during the interview, even if your body is rebelling and making it hard for you to do your job.

Avoid fidgeting throughout the interview.

Refrain from fidgeting throughout the interview since this could indicate that you are extremely nervous and make things more difficult for you. To avoid making any unintentional movements, try to stay as still as you can in your seat. Always be aware of your posture, and maintain your feet facing front.

Hit the pause/play button.

Another thing you should do is hit the pause button if you think you might stray from your intended path. Imagine that you are responding to a question where you are required to discuss the specifics of your prior work experience. You don't want to ramble on and on about it in the incorrect way. You can prevent yourself from providing an excessively detailed response to a question by pressing the pause button. If you want to respond to a question completely and concisely, attempt to state only what is necessary and omit any extraneous details. Remind yourself not to go any farther. Let's examine a specific illustration of this:

Frank is responding to a query during an interview. He's in the center of it, exactly. "Frank, tell me about your previous manager," the interviewer asks. How did he or she fare? Frank continues, "Well, she was a micromanager, and that was pretty tough to handle at times, but I did the best I could to work with her." She could also be really disorganized at times, but I could tell that her job was difficult. He held his tongue when he wanted to say, "She was really messy and interrupted my schedule." She constantly irritated me, which is why I became so angry with her. She destroyed my life by spreading a lot of rumors about me as well.

You don't want to divulge excessive details. That would divulge more information than is necessary. As a result, you should limit your responses to being succinct and direct rather than losing your cool and criticising someone in the middle of the interview. It will only be a catastrophic circumstance. Despite the fact that you are discussing a challenging circumstance you encountered with a former supervisor, make an effort to be upbeat.

How To Make Worrying Useful

Anxiety is a common trait among people with GAD, although it doesn't seem to help them much. As such, they are still concerned. Furthermore, individuals still worry even after taking actions that ought to lessen their need for concern. For instance, they can be concerned about managing a duty that is coming up. They appear to be more prepared than most individuals who worry about these things, but it does not make much difference. Even with the action, they are still concerned. People are still very concerned even after taking the necessary precautions, and their level of concern is still rather high.

Anxiety, by itself, achieves nothing. Behavior is the only thing that produces results. Thus, even though you have caused discomfort by worrying about an impending occurrence, worrying does not lessen the event's danger. Behavior that gets you ready for the scenario lowers the risk. For instance, you can prepare yourself by doing your homework and coming prepared with answers to inquiries about how you fit into the firm if you are nervous before a job interview.

Worrying appears to persist in generalized anxiety disorder, maybe because the behavioral component is frequently absent. As is often the case, thinking about possible hazards makes us more anxious, which drives us to take actions that lower the risk and, in turn, lower our anxiety. Anxiety is persistent in generalized anxiety disorder, partly because there is a cause for the anxiety. Nothing has changed; the individual worried but didn't spend much time acting on it. Because worrying makes us feel as though we are preparing, worrying gives the impression that something is being done. However, to lessen worry, we must use its ability to motivate us to take action. Several actions can be considered effective depending on the circumstances and our resources. It's critical to keep activity from being impeded by the notion of perfection. Procrastination, which impedes all productive action, can result from perfectionism. Rather than insisting on being ready for every scenario, the objective should be to prepare as much as feasible.

Anxiety has the power to immobilize behavior. We cannot act because we are so consumed by our fear and paralyzed by the thought that we are unprepared to handle the problems. As such, we are no better prepared than we were before. Therefore, there is no need to ease our concerns. Furthermore, there is even more cause for concern because we are closer to the possible threat, or the threat is more plausible. As our anxiety grows, so does our capacity to take action to lessen the real risk.

Fish oil supplements

Fish oil is wonderful to aid with anxiety. The capsules are available at any pharmacy. They are frequently in the vitamin aisle. Fish oil does not taste very pleasant, so it is a good idea to acquire it in a capsule and take it down with water. This will help decrease tension; taking fish oil capsules in the morning is a good idea before heading out to work. If you already consume a lot of fish, you do not need to take fish oil capsules. Salmon, sardines, and even mussels are great oily fish to replace the capsules. You want to eat different varieties of fish that are abundant in fatty acids to acquire the required dose.

Kava kava

Getting kava pills will assist with anxiety. It is a potent herb, so be careful to take this kava capsule occasionally and do not use it daily. If you are suffering from anxiety and sadness, this is an excellent herb to turn to for relief. This herb has been shown to lower anxiety and despair substantially. You can put kava in your hot tea. It tastes extremely wonderful, although it does make your tongue a bit numb. I think this herb is the most useful for anxiety, although there have been studies showing that people who take alcohol daily or people who have liver problems have had trouble with this herb.

Skullcap Skullcap is particularly useful for anyone with significant anxiety, muscle tension, and jaw clenching. It is reported to aid with anxiety, sleeplessness, excessive cholesterol, allergies, and skin infections. This plant will be found as a pill and might be store-bought at any medicine or vitamin store. A skullcap is known as a mint. Thus, this will also be an excellent herb to throw into your hot tea to help alleviate anxiety.

Valerian

This herb has been known as effective but should be consumed for up to three weeks after consuming this herb. An adverse effect of taking valerian could be acquiring a headache. Valerian is a sedative for the brain and neurological system. Taking valerian before bed would help, as it makes you drowsy. You may find these valerian capsules at your local drug shop.

Uncertainty In Partnerships

What is Insecure About?

Feelings of inadequacy, or not being strong enough, and uncertainty are traits of insecurity. It makes you worry about your goals, relationships, and ability to handle particular situations.

Everyone has experienced insecurity at some point in their lives. It can have multiple causes and present itself in any area of life. It could be the consequence of a traumatic event or encounter, social conditioning (picking up rules by seeing others), or local environments like the workplace, home, or school.

It could also result from an overall feeling of insecurity. Individuals who experience unpredictable disruptions in their daily lives are more likely to experience feelings of insecurity regarding their routines and chances. Conversely, insecurity is not attributable to any one external factor. Rather, it can be mistakenly believed to be a mental illness or a shift in brain chemistry. Understanding the nature of insecurities will help you deal with your own and help others.

Kinds of Uncertainties

There are several potential places where insecurity may arise. Moreover, insecurity frequently affects other facets of life. However, some types of insecurity are more prevalent than others.

Partnership Uncertainty

Attachments and relationships are among the main causes of insecurity. The creation of attachment theory was prompted by the capacity to connect attachment patterns in early childhood to patterns and goals in future relationships. When parents or grandparents—a child's primary attachment figures—do not always respond and support them, the youngster experiences insecurity, forms unfavorable relationships or self-images, and experiences more emotional discomfort and maladjustment as they age.

It is not necessary for relationship or commitment-related fears to originate in childhood. They will happen if someone's experience or insecurities compromise their confidence in their closest relationships.

Workplace Uncertainty

You are insecure when you are concerned about the stability of your employment or the continuation of the benefits that come with it. worries about how well you're performing at work and worries about external factors like the economy, market dynamics, conflict at work, or the possibility of a company restructuring or closing. Extreme mental health problems are caused by high unemployment rates and casual labor, which increase job insecurity nationally.

Body Image Concerns

One common cause of insecurity is one's body image. Many people worry about whether they satisfy a predetermined standard and are self-conscious about how they look. There is not always a connection between physical attractiveness, true physical health, or body insecurities. People with various physique shapes can experience this type of insecurity.

Anxiety and Social Insecurity

How our co-workers perceive us and how simple it is to communicate with them can also be a source of unease. This insecurity may remain a mild, recurrent problem, or it may become a full-blown social anxiety disorder or social phobia.